Fifty Prayers

KARL BARTH

Translated by
David Carl Stassen

Westminster John Knox Press
LOUISVILLE • LONDON

Translated by David Carl Stassen from the German *Fünfzig Gebete* published in 2005 by Theologischer Verlag Zürich, Zürich, Switzerland

Book design by Drew Stevens
Cover design by Lisa Buckley

First edition
Published by Westminster John Knox Press
Louisville, Kentucky

This book is printed on acid-free paper that meets the American National Standards Institute Z39.48 standard. ♾

PRINTED IN THE UNITED STATES OF AMERICA

08 09 10 11 12 13 14 15 16 17 — 10 9 8 7 6 5 4 3 2 1

Library of Congress Cataloging-in-Publication Data

Barth, Karl, 1886–1968.
   [Fünfzig Gebete. English]
   Fifty prayers / Karl Barth ; translated by David Carl Stassen. — 1st ed.
      p. cm.
   ISBN 978-0-664-23153-8 (alk. paper)
   1. Prayers. 2. Church year—Prayers and devotions. I. Title.
   BV245.B328 2008
   242.8—dc22

                                                                    2007031688

CONTENTS

With the exception of a few unprinted prayers, the prayers in this volume are taken from Karl Barth, *Predigten 1954–1967,* third edition (Zürich: Theologischer Verlag Zürich, 2003).

In this volume are collected sermons and prayers of Karl Barth that were once contained in the now-out-of-print volumes of sermons *Fürchte dich nicht* and *Dem Gefangenen Befreiung.*

FOREWORD

I could certainly not have dreamed in the earlier decades of my life that another little book of prayers would come out under my name. In my youth, I had a dislike for all manner of worship formalities. And only a few years ago, the well-known leader of the Alpirsbach Movement, whom I rather like, said of me that I understand nothing of liturgy. Indeed, when I had to preach before the "altars" of the German churches, I moved with uncertainty. In my old Bonn days, I even once stood behind the "altar" instead of in front of it, in a decided sense of my own power, but I could not do that a second time. (Now, of course, even the Roman Mass is often celebrated from there!) For other reasons, my friend Günther Dehn made me leave the Poppelsdorf church after the war with the harsh censure "Preaching: A. Liturgy: D." And so, with the contents of this little book, I have entered into the society of true liturgy only through a back door.

For a long time I never felt good when before

and after my sermons I thought I should, or was allowed, to keep to the order of the usual liturgical books halfway here and there (or simply out of laziness?). I was disturbed by the lack of functional relationships, but also by the inorganic relationship between the archaic or even the modern language of these prayers and the language of my sermons. For a while, I sought help by replacing the petitions of the order of liturgy not with extemporaneous prayers (I have never dared to risk such a thing), but with freely bringing together biblical passages from the Psalms. Only in more recent years did I begin to set forth such texts, first for the end and later for the beginning of the main part of the worship service, within the context of preparing for the sermons themselves.

These sermons, together with the prayers, have been published in the collections *Fürchte dich nicht* and *Dem Gefangenen Befreiung*. I have always resisted the idea the sermons would be published without the prayers that went with them. In short, the considerations that guided me were these: The worship service, as the center of the entire life of the community, must be presented as a whole, a whole of calling on the gracious God. Following the greeting of the community as the people of this God, the worship begins with the common singing, which I think is not seen as being as important as it truly is. It continues with the pronouncement of the community's thanks, its penance, and its special petition for God's presence and support in the special act of gathering for worship, by the member of the community who serves as the leader of the action. It ascends to the sermon, in which the call to explanation and application of the Scripture passage (better short than long!) is spoken and proclaimed. From here, it descends to the final prayer, in which the proclamation of the sermon is briefly summarized (with a direct call to God), but in which the worship service is possibly opened, above all, as an outstretched petition to the outside, to all other people, to the rest of the church and the world (is this not too often neglected?). In the second common singing, the assembly makes this final prayer their own. They are dismissed by the serving community member with the giving of the blessing, "The LORD bless you and keep you . . ." (not us!). (If it were up to me, then this formula would also be used for the services of baptism and Holy Communion.) The spice for all parts of all spiritual and theological sayings should consist in brevity!

The prayers that are collected in this little book are formulated within this context. The divisions into the "liturgical year" in which they appear and the titles for the various divisions are not mine. But I would certainly approve of them. Those elements, especially of petition, that are too bound to the time they were prayed can be omitted here (I am thinking specifically of prayers for the Swiss Army that was often guarding the border during the time of war, and also in his time for the just-chosen Pope John XXIII).

I cannot expect that the essence and structure of the worship service that I have just sketched out for clarification will meet with general acceptance.

But it may be—and this was the thought of the friends who troubled themselves with the collection and publication of these prayers—that the prayers might prove to be useful, even without the presupposition of my perhaps too-Reformed "liturgical" conception. My vision is not that the prayers, such as they are, will simply be taken over by communities and preachers, but rather that they might be read as a stimulus for earnest consideration. Might the worship leader, in and with the assembled community, use the prayers as the object of his own special, careful attention and work? The prayers might also be welcome here and there for personal and private use.

Basel, Advent 1962   Karl Barth

You Know Who We Are

1 Lord, our God, you know who we are: People with good and bad consciences; satisfied and dissatisfied, sure and unsure people; Christians out of conviction and Christians out of habit; believers, half-believers, and unbelievers.

You know where we come from: from our circle of relatives, friends, and acquaintances, or from great loneliness; from lives of quiet leisure, or from all manner of embarrassment and distress; from ordered, tense, or destroyed family relationships; from the inner circle, or from the fringes of the Christian community.

But now we all stand before you: in all our inequality equal in this, that we are all in the wrong before you and among each other; that we all must die some day; that we all would be lost without your grace; but also in that your grace is promised to and turned toward all of us through your beloved Son, our Lord, Jesus Christ.

We are here together in order to praise you by allowing you to speak to us. We ask that this might happen in this hour in the name of your Son, our Lord. Amen.

2 Dear Father in heaven, we thank you for the eternal, living, saving Word that in Jesus you have spoken and continue to speak to us human beings. Do not allow us to hear it only in a cursory fashion and to be too lazy to obey it. Do not let us fall, but remain near each one of us with your comfort, and between each of us and our fellow human beings with your peace. Let dawn continue to break a little in our hearts, in this institution, at home with those who are dear to us, in this city, in our nation, and throughout the whole earth. You know the errors and misdeeds that make our current situation once again so dark and dangerous on all sides. Let a fresh wind blow through it, that might at least scatter the thickest fog from the heads of those who rule this world, but also from the heads of the peoples who permit themselves to be ruled, and above all from the heads of those who make public opinion. And have mercy on all of those who are sick in body and in spirit, the many for whom life is suffering, those who are lost and confused through their own or others' fault, those who have no human friends or helpers. Show our youth also what true freedom and genuine joy are, and do not leave the old and the dying without the hope of the resurrection and eternal life. But you are the first, who are concerned about our sorrows, and you are the only one who can turn them to good. We thus can and want only to lift our eyes up toward you. Our help comes from you, who made heaven and earth. Amen.

Advent: Your Gift to Receive

3 Lord, may you now let us this year once more approach the light, celebration, and joy of Christmas Day that brings us face to face with the greatest thing there is: your love, with which you so loved the world that you gave your only Son, so that all of us may believe in him and therefore not be lost, but may have eternal life.

What could we possibly bring and give to you? So much darkness in our human relationships and in our own hearts! So many confused thoughts, so much coldness and defiance, so much carelessness and hatred! So much over which you cannot rejoice, that separates us from one another and certainly cannot help us! So much that runs directly against the message of Christmas!

What should you possibly do with such gifts? And what are you to do with such people as we all are? But all of this is precisely what you want to receive from us and take from us at Christmas—the whole pile of rubbish and ourselves, just as we are—in order to give us in return Jesus, our Savior, and in him a new heaven and a new earth, new hearts and a new desire, new clarity and a new hope for us and for all people.

Be among us as we once again, on this final Sunday before the celebration, together prepare to receive him as your gift! Make it so that we may rightly speak, hear, and pray, in proper, thankful amazement about everything that you have in mind for all of us, that you have already decided regarding all of us, and that you have already done for all of us! Amen.

4 Lord, our God and Father, give to many, to all, and to us as well, that we may celebrate Christmas like this: that in complete thankfulness, utter humility, and then complete joy and confidence we may come to the one whom you have sent, and in whom you yourself have come to us. Clean out the many things in us that, now that the hour has come, have become impossible for us, can no longer belong to us, may, must, and will fall away from us, by virtue of your beloved Son, our Lord and Savior, entering into our midst and creating order.

Have mercy also on all of those who either do not yet or do not fully know you and your kingdom, who perhaps once knew everything and have either forgotten, misunderstood, or even denied it! Have mercy on all of humankind, who today are once again especially plagued, threatened, and haunted by so much foolishness! Enlighten the thoughts of those in both the East and the West who are in power and who, as appears to be the case, are today in complete confusion and despair! Give the rulers and representatives of the people, the judges, teachers, and bureaucrats, give even the newspaper reporters in our homeland, the insight and sobriety that are necessary for their responsible work! Place the right, necessary, and helpful words on the lips of those who have to preach during this Christmas season, and open then also the ears and hearts of those who hear them! Comfort and encourage those who are sick, both in body and spirit, in the hospitals, as well as the prisoners, and those who are distressed, abandoned, or despairing! Help them with what alone can truly help them and all of us: the clarity of your Word and the quiet work of your Holy Spirit.

We thank you that we are permitted to know that we do not pray and will never pray to you in vain. We thank you that you have let your light rise, that it shines in the darkness, and that the darkness will not overcome it. We thank you that you are our God, and that we may be your people. Amen.

Christmas: Hope for the Whole World

5 Dear heavenly Father, because we are here with one another in order to rejoice over the fact that your dear Son for us became a human and our brother, we earnestly beg of you to tell us yourself what great grace, well-being, and help you have prepared for all of us in him.

Open our ears and our understanding, in order that we may grasp that in him there is forgiveness for all of our sins, the seed and strength of a new life, comfort and admonition in life and in death, and hope for the whole world! Create in us the good spirit of freedom humbly and bravely to come to your Son, who comes to us!

Do this today in all of Christendom and in the world, that there may be many who break through all of the vain externalities of these festive days and celebrate a good Christmas with us. Amen.

6 Lord our God, you are great, high, and holy over us and over all people. And indeed, you are so great that you have not forgotten us, have

not left us alone, and despite all that might testify against us, you have not rejected us. Now, in your dear Son, Jesus Christ, our Lord, you have given us nothing less than yourself and all that is yours. We thank you that, as long as we live and in eternity, we may be your guests at the table of your grace.

We now spread before you everything that troubles us: our mistakes and attempts to overreach, our sorrows, cares, rebellion, and bitterness—our whole hearts and lives that you know better than we do. We place all of this into the trustworthy hands that in our Savior you have stretched out toward us. Take us as we are, hold up the weak among us, and make the poor among us rich from your fullness!

And so, let your friendliness shine over us and over all who are in prison or suffering and over those who are sick or near death. To those who judge, give the spirit of justice; to those who rule in the world, give something of your wisdom, that they may be mindful of peace on earth. Give clarity and courage to those who must proclaim your Word, both here and in missions.

And now we bring everything together, in that we call on you, as the Savior has allowed and promised us:

> Our Father, who art in heaven,
> hallowed be thy name,
> thy kingdom come,
> thy will be done,
> on earth as it is in heaven.

Give us this day our daily bread;
and forgive us our debts,
as we forgive our debtors,
and lead us not into temptation,
but deliver us from evil.
For thine is the kingdom,
and the power, and the glory,
forever.
Amen.

7 Lord our God, you have humbled yourself, that we may be exalted. You became poor, that we may become rich. You came to us, that we may come to you. You became a human being like us, that we may be drawn into participation in your eternal life: All of this from your free, undeserved grace; all of this in your dear Son, our Lord and Savior, Jesus Christ.

We are gathered here, in view of this mystery and wonder, to pray to you, praise you, and to proclaim and hear your Word. But we know that we cannot do these things under our own power, that it is you who free us to lift our hearts and thoughts to you. So we ask you to come now into our midst! Show us and open to us the path to you through your Holy Spirit, so that we may see with our own eyes your light that has come into the world, in order that our lives may indeed be witnesses to you. Amen.

8 Dear Father, through Jesus Christ, our Lord, make good what we fail to do well, even this worship service in all of its inadequacy and the

many other Christmas celebrations that we will go to, whether comprehending or failing to comprehend! You can make water flow from the rock, transform water into wine, and raise up children for Abraham from these very stones—all in the great, inconceivable faithfulness that you have sworn to your people and have kept again and again. We thank you that this faithfulness shines in the gospel, and that we may hold on to it in all circumstances. Do not allow us to harden ourselves to it! Continually awaken us from the sleep of indifference and the bad dreams of our pious and impious passions and desires! Do not tire of continually guiding us back onto your path!

Defend against the foolish works of the Cold War and the mutual threat through which the peoples of the world today find themselves in such frightful danger. Give to the rulers and those who carry responsibility for public opinion the new wisdom, patience, and decisiveness that are required today, in order to fashion and preserve justice for all in your good world! We ask that whatever is done in our city, our church, our university, and our schools may not happen without your light or without your blessing for the true well-being of all, and to your glory. We ask you, above all, for the many for whom it must be difficult to celebrate Christmas now: for the poor, both known and unknown; for those who are aging alone; for those who are physically and mentally ill; and for the prisoners; that, despite everything, it may be a little brighter for them! Finally, we beg of you concerning those of us both near and far away, as well as for all people, that you may hold your hand graciously over our lives and over our deaths.

Lord, have mercy on us! Your name be praised, now and forevermore! Amen.

9 Lord our God, you wanted to live not only in heaven, but also with us, here on earth; not only to be high and great, but also to be small and lowly, as we are; not only to rule, but also to serve us; not only to be God in eternity, but also to be born as a person, to live, and to die.

In your dear Son, our Savior Jesus Christ, you have given us none other than yourself, that we may wholly belong to you. This affects all of us, and none of us has deserved this. What remains for us to do but to wonder, to rejoice, to be thankful, and to hold fast to what you have done for us?

We ask you to let this be the case in this hour, among us and in all of us! Let us become a proper Christmas community in honest, open, and willing praying and singing, speaking and hearing, and let us in great hunger be a proper Communion community! Amen.

10 Lord our God, when we are afraid, do not permit us to doubt! When we are disappointed, let us not become bitter! When we have fallen, do not leave us lying down! When we have come to the end of our understanding and our powers, do not leave us to die! No, let us then feel your nearness and your love, that you have promised to those whose hearts are humble and broken,

and who fear your Word. Your Son has come to all people, just as he has come to all who bear heavy burdens. Because we are all so burdened, he was born in the manger, and he died on the cross. Lord, awaken us all and keep us all awake to this knowledge and to this confession.

And now, we think of all of the darkness and suffering in this time of ours, of the many errors and misunderstandings with which we struggle, of all of the hardship that so many must carry without comfort, of all of the great dangers with which the world is threatened, without any clue as to how to deal with them. We think of the physically and the mentally ill, the poor, the downtrodden, the oppressed, those who are suffering unjustly, of the children who have no parents, or who have no good parents. We also think of all who are called to help as much as people can help: the leaders of our nation and of all other nations, the judges and officials, the teachers and educators, those who write books and newspapers, the doctors and nurses in the hospitals, and those who proclaim your Word in the different churches and communities both near and far. We think of all of these with the prayer that the light of Christmas might shine on them and on us far more brightly than before, so that they and we may be helped. All of this in the name of the Savior, in whom you have already answered us and will continually answer us. Amen.

Year's End

11 Lord our God, our years come and go. We ourselves live and die. But you are and remain. Your rule and your faithfulness, your justice and your mercy, have no beginning and no end. You are thus the origin and the aim of our lives. You are thus the judge of our thoughts, words, and deeds.

We are sorry that today we can only confess that so often, right up to this very hour and continually anew, we have forgotten, denied, and offended you. But today your Word—through which you allow us to recognize that you are our Father and we are your children, because your dear Son, Jesus Christ, became incarnate for us, died, and was raised, and is our brother—enlightens and comforts us.

We thank you that now, on this final Sunday of the year, we may yet again proclaim and hear this joyful message. Make us free to say the right thing, and to hear it properly, so that this hour may bring you honor and all of us peace and salvation. Amen.

12 Lord, our Father, you tell us today as you did yesterday, and you will tell us tomorrow as you have today, that you have always loved us and have drawn us to yourself out of pure goodness. We hear you; grant that we hear you correctly! We believe; help our unbelief! We want to obey you; bring an end to everything that is much too weak and much too hard in us, that we may truly and properly obey You! We trust you; cast out all the ghosts from our heads and hearts, that we may wholly and happily trust you! We run to you for shelter; let us earnestly leave behind everything that must be left behind, and let us look ahead and move forward in bright confidence!

Help all who are in this house; all those in this city and in the whole wide world who are in error, who are sorrowful, bitter, and confused; all prisoners; those who are sick in the hospitals and mental hospitals; those in politics who have positions of leadership; those who call out for bread, justice, and freedom; and those nations that wage war, whether with or without reason; the teachers and instructors and the children who are entrusted to them; the churches, regardless of direction or persuasion, that they may guard and spread the pure light of your Word.

We see so much, both near and far, that grieves and discourages us, and that also makes us angry and indifferent. But in you, there is complete order, peace, freedom, and joy. You were the hope for us and for the whole world in the old year, and you will also be the same in the new year. We lift our hearts—no, you be the one to lift our hearts to you! To you, the Father, the Son, and the Holy Spirit, be the honor, yesterday, today, tomorrow, and forever. Amen.

13 Lord, God of heaven and earth, here we are once again, one last time at the end of the year, together to hear what you have said to us and say again and again, together to praise you as well as we can, together to call on you to give us what only you can give us.

We need forgiveness for the innumerable things that we have done wrong this year, and we need light in the great darkness that surrounds and fills us in these last hours of the year. We need new courage and new strength to move forward from where we are now and continue toward the goal that you have set for us. We need much greater faith in your promises, much stronger hope in your gracious actions, and much more love for you and for our neighbors. These are our New Year's wishes, which only you can fulfill.

Be then among us even in this hour! Show us again that you are not far from us all and from each of us, but that you are near and will hear our petitions, and that you will be far better than we could imagine or conceive. And on this evening, for the many others who are at their wits' end without you, be the faithful God who was, and is, and will be for the whole world! Amen.

14 Lord, our dear God, we thank you that you remain as you are and that your years have no end; that you give to us and will give to us; that

your Word remains, in which *your* heart is opened and speaks to *our* hearts. Give us the freedom to cling to it and it alone where everything else fails. And now in this freedom, let us today take the final steps of the old year and tomorrow the first steps of the new year, as well as all further steps into whatever future is granted us, whether short or long!

Continually enlighten and awaken to this same freedom new people—old and young, high and lowly, clever and foolish—that they may be witnesses of what remains in eternity! Give a little, or perhaps a great deal, of the dawning light of eternity to the prisons in all nations, to the clinics and schools, to the council chambers and editorial offices, to all of the places where people suffer and work, speak and make decisions, and so easily forget that you rule and that they are responsible to you. And give some of this dawning light to the hearts of those close to us, as well as to those known and unknown to us, to the poor, the abandoned, the confused, the hungry, the sick, and the dying! May it not fail us either, whenever the hour of our death may come!

Great God, we praise you. Our hope is in you alone. Let us not be lost! Amen.

Epiphany: Awaken Us

15 Lord our God, we thank you that we can gather together in this hour, to call on you, to bring everything that moves us before you, together to hear the joyful message of the world's salvation, to glorify you.

Come to us now! Awaken us! Give us your light! Be our Teacher and Comforter! Speak to each of us, so that we may hear just what we need and what will help us!

And so, be gracious to all others everywhere who have gathered together as your community! Preserve them and us by your Word! Protect them and us from hypocrisy, error, boredom, and distraction! Give them and us knowledge and hope, a clear witness, and joyful hearts, through Jesus Christ, our Lord. Amen.

16 Lord, our God, dear Father, you have loved the world, in that you sent your only begotten Son, so that all who believe in him will not perish, but have eternal life. Write this on our hearts

and minds now, and enlighten our understanding that in his death, the old person in each of us is also dead, and that in his resurrection, the new person is born in each of us. Teach us to believe and in faith to go from death to life. You loved us first. Do not leave us in lovelessness, in indecisiveness, and in the cold.

We ask that you empower your community everywhere, and that you preserve and renew it, that it may joyfully and clearly proclaim your name, your will, and your kingdom. We ask that among our time's troubled humanity you make living and fruitful the free witness of the old, which must pass, and of the new, which must grow. We ask that all those who rule may be advised, may decide, and may act responsibly before you. We ask that you bless the mission to the unbelievers, the education of the youth, and the care of all the oppressed and suffering through the presence and the light of your Spirit. We ask for comfort and help for all the sick, the prisoners, the abandoned, and the confused. We ask that each one of us may be mindful of your eternal faithfulness for the sake of Jesus Christ. Amen.

The Passion

17 Lord, God, our Father, we thank you that here with each other we can call on you and listen to you. Before you, we are all equal. You know the life, thoughts, path, and heart of each of us, down to the smallest and most hidden detail, and before your eyes none is righteous, no, not one. But you have not forgotten, rejected, or condemned a single one of us. Quite the opposite: you love each one of us; you know what we need, will grant it to us, will look at nothing but the empty hands that we stretch out to you, in order that they might be filled—not sparingly, but richly. In the suffering and death of Jesus, your dear Son, you were gracious and exceedingly helpful when you took our place, you took our darkness and laments on yourself, and you have made us free to come to your light and rejoice as your children.

In his name, we ask that you now give each of us something of your good Holy Spirit, so that in this hour we may understand you, ourselves, and each other a little better, and that thereby we may be quickened and encouraged to take a step forward along the path that you have set for all of us, whether we know it or not—both then, as Jesus, hanging on the cross, bowed his head and died, and from all eternity. Amen.

18 Lord our God, we praise you and thank you that you, in your dear Son, in mercy beyond understanding, would humble yourself so much for our sakes, in order that in him we may be so highly exalted for your sake. We praise you and thank you for this mighty decision regarding your people Israel and the pagan nations from which you called our ancestors. We praise you and thank you for all of your gracious election and calling, that you are also the God of the rejected and the uncalled, and that you never cease to deal with each one of us in a fatherly and righteous manner. Let us never tire of recognizing you and praying to you in all of these mysteries, that we may in faith lay hold of your Word, through which you magnify your honor and give us, with eternal blessing, peace and joy, even in this life. We pray for your church here and in all nations, for the sleeping church, that it may awaken; for the persecuted church, that it may continually rejoice and be assured of what it has in you; and for the confessing church, that it may live not for its own sake, but for your glory.

We pray for the rulers and the authorities all over the world: for the good ones, that you may preserve them; and for the bad ones, that you may either turn their hearts or put an end to their power, all according to your will; and for everyone, that you may advise them that they are and must remain your servants.

We pray that all tyranny and disorder may be fended off, and that all oppressed nations and people may be granted justice.

We pray for the poor, the sick, the prisoners, the helpless, and the troubled, for all who suffer — perhaps from something only you know — that you yourself may comfort them with the hope of your kingdom. Amen.

Good Friday

19 Lord our God, we are gathered here on this day to consider how you have carried out your good, firm will for the world and for all of us, by allowing our Lord Jesus Christ, your dear Son, to be captured that we might be free; to be found guilty that we might be found innocent; to suffer that we might rejoice; and to be given over to death that we might live forever.

Under our own power, we could only be lost. And we have not deserved such a rescue—no, not one of us. But in the inconceivable greatness of your mercy, you have shared in our sin and our poverty, in order to do such a great thing for us. How else could we thank you but to grasp, take up, and acknowledge this great thing? How else should this happen, but that the same living Savior who suffered for us, was crucified, died, was buried, and was also raised up, should now come into our midst, speak to our hearts and minds, open us to your love, and guide us to trust in it completely and to live by it and by it alone.

So we ask you in all humility, but also in all confidence, that this happen in the power of your Holy Spirit. Amen.

20 Lord our God, merciful and almighty Father, you loved this poor world so much that you allowed your own dear Son to take such a wonderful path for its liberation and for the liberation of us all! For you, this was the right path, and there was no other; and so it should be for us as well. And if this is indeed the case—that we find freedom only through him and in communion with him, that we reach the heights only by going through the depths, that we find joy only through suffering, and that we come to life only through death—then we wish to accept this as your good and proper order.

Help us, that there may always be some who recognize your path with Jesus and with us, and that they may find peace in the way you have ordered things, here in this house and everywhere else all over the world where the death of our Lord is considered, even where it is either not thought of at all, or where it is not thought of rightly. You have access to those people whom we do not see or know, who nevertheless have full access to you.

In this certainty, we now think of the physically and mentally ill, the poor and the sad, those who are in error or confusion of any kind. In this certainty, we ask for the spirit of wisdom for all those who hold positions of responsibility within the church and the state, that they may properly discuss, advise, decide, judge, and command; for the workers and their bosses; for the teachers and their students; for the people who write books and newspapers; and for those who read them. All of them, all of us find it necessary that in the face of our Lord's cross, we should all be prayed for, and that, in the face of his cross, we should pray for each other! And how holy and friendly you are, that we can hold on to the fact that every righteous prayer is heard by you.

We thank you that Jesus lives and that we can live with him. And finally, we thank you that, as a sign of this, we all can now receive Holy Communion with one another. Amen.

Easter: You Are the Life

21 Lord, our God, here we are gathered, before you and with one another, to celebrate Easter, the day on which you revealed your dear Son, our Lord Jesus Christ, as the living Savior who took upon himself all of our sins and, with them, all of our human poverty and even death itself, paid the penance and suffered in our place, and once for all and forevermore conquered them all and set them all aside.

We know well how it is with us, and you know it better still. But we come, and we thank you for the freedom that we have to turn our eyes away from ourselves and toward you, who have done such a thing for the world and for us all.

Let us now speak and hear in an upright fashion, that it may be your true Word that reigns, moves, and fills this hour; that it may comfort, encourage, and admonish all of us; that even our poor praise may please you!

Let this come to pass among us, as well as

everywhere else in the city and in the nation, both near and far, wherever people gather today to hear and grasp the promise of the resurrection and the life. Look on your people with grace! Amen.

22 Lord, God our Father, through Jesus Christ, your Son, in the power of your Holy Spirit, give light to our eyes, that we may see your light, the brightly shining light of reconciliation! For this is the greatest sickness, when one cannot see the light, even during the day. Free us from this sickness, us and all Christians who celebrate Easter either well or poorly, the entire human community, both near and far, who are again and again being confused and endangered anew!

Bless what comes to pass in this church and in the other churches and communities that are now still separated from us, that it may be a testimony to your name, your kingdom, and your will! Reign also over all of the various concerns of the government authorities, administrations, and courts here and all over the world! Strengthen the teachers in consideration of their high task for the growing generation; the people who write newspapers, conscious of their grave responsibility for the public opinion that they influence; the doctors and nurses, for genuine attentiveness to the needs of those who are in their care! Substitute your comfort, your counsel, and your help for all that would accuse the many lonely, poor, sick, and confused among us! And let your mercy be apparent and powerful to all who are here in this house, along with their families!

We place ourselves and all that we lack and that the world requires in your hands. Our hope is in you. We trust in you. You have never let your people be put to shame, whenever they earnestly called on you. What you have begun, you will surely finish. Amen.

23 Lord God, our Father, you are the light in which there is no darkness. And now you have kindled in us a light that can never be extinguished and that will ultimately drive out all darkness. You are the love that knows no coldness. And now you have loved even us and freed us to love you and each other. You are the life that mocks death. And now you have given us access to this eternal life. You have done all this in Jesus Christ, your Son, our brother.

Do not let us—let none of us—remain dull and indifferent to your gift and revelation. Let us on this Easter morning see at least something of the riches of your goodness; let it enter into our hearts and minds, and let it enlighten us, uphold us, comfort us, and admonish us!

None of us is a great Christian; rather, we are all very small Christians. But your grace is sufficient for us. Awaken us to the small joy and thankfulness that we are capable of, the timid faith that we bring, the incomplete obedience that we cannot refuse—to the hope in the greatness, wholeness, and completeness that you have prepared for us in the death of our Lord, Jesus Christ, and that you have promised us in his resurrection from the dead. We ask that this hour may serve that purpose. Amen.

24 Our one God, our only God, fierce in your goodness, holy and mighty in all that you do, we come yet again to you as people who have nothing to offer you but the confession that we want to live from your great, free mercy. We thank you that you invite and encourage us to come to such a place. You do not forget us; let us not forget you! You do not tire; let us not grow weary! You choose and desire what is right and wholesome for each one of us; protect us from our willful wants and desires!

But we also want to bring before you the requests, questions, and needs of many others. Consider all those, whether in this house or elsewhere, who are in prison! Consider also our families both near and far! Comfort and quicken all those who are physically and mentally ill, all those in need, and especially those who have no human friends or helpers! Help the refugees, the oppressed, and all those who suffer injustice throughout the world! Instruct those who teach, and rule over those who are destined and called to rule! Make for your gospel joyful and courageous witnesses in all the churches, including the Catholic church and the free communities! Accompany and enlighten the missionaries and the young congregations that they wish to serve! Let all of those who hope in you work while it is day, and give good fruit to the honest concerns of all those who either do not know you, do not know you yet, or do not know you properly! You hear those who have upright hearts. Make us upright, that you may also hear us!

You were God from eternity, you are God, and you will be God. We rejoice that we can build on you and trust in you. Amen.

The Ascension:
To Believe, to Love,
and to Hope

25 Lord, our God, our Father, through your Son, who became our brother, you call out to us: Return again, children of men! Lift up your hearts! Seek what is above! So, you have called us together on this morning. And here we are, each one of us with a life that does not belong to us, but to you, a life that is completely in your hand; each of us with our small and great sins, for which there is forgiveness only in you; each of us with our concerns, which only you can transform into joy. Yet each of us also has our own, quiet hope, that you may show yourself to be our almighty, good, and gracious God.

We know that one thing only can please you and give you honor: to earnestly ask for your Spirit, earnestly seek your truth, and earnestly desire your presence and your direction. But we know that even this can be only your work in us. Lord, awaken us, that we may be awake!

So grant that in this hour all may happen properly: our prayer and singing, our speaking and hearing, and our celebration of Holy Communion. Grant this to all who this day desire to celebrate together the ascension of our Lord, Jesus Christ; also to the sick people in the hospitals, the confused people, and the many, many people who perhaps simply do not know that in truth, they also are imprisoned, sick, and confused, who perhaps cannot yet hear that you are their comfort, their confidence, and their Savior. Let a light shine on them, and on us as well, through Jesus Christ, our Lord. Amen.

26 Lord, our God, our Father in Jesus Christ, your Son, and our brother, we thank you that everything is as we have now again attempted to say and hear. We are sorry that so often we have been blind and deaf to the light of your Word. And we are sorry for all of the sin in our lives that this has caused. And because we know well that without you we would be continually lost, we ask that you not cease to touch us with your Holy Spirit, to awaken us, and to make us alert, humble, and brave. We do not ask this for each one of us individually, but we ask this for one another, all those who are in this house, for all prisoners in the world, for all who are suffering or ill in body or spirit, for the homeless and the downtrodden, and also for all those whose concerns and needs are hidden from us, but not from you. We ask this also for those close to us, for all parents, teachers, and students, for the people who hold positions of responsibility in the state, the administration, and the court, and for the preachers and ministers of your gospel.

Help them and all of us to bear what must be borne; but also, above all, to think, say, and do what is right; to believe, to love, and to hope in the great riches that you will give to them and to us. Amen.

Pentecost: Give Us Your Spirit

27 Lord, our God, we come into your presence, in adoration of your majesty, in recognition of our unworthiness, and in gratitude for all of your good gifts that you continually grant us in body and spirit. We thank you especially for this Sunday and celebration day, on which we may consider how your dear Son, our Lord Jesus Christ, after he returned to you, did not leave us orphaned, but wanted to be present and remain with us in the Holy Spirit, the Comforter and Teacher, who gives us life, until he himself returns in his glory. And now, help us rightly to recognize you and praise you in this good work of yours, that your Word might rightly be proclaimed and heard, both here in this place and everywhere where your people call on you. Sanctify and bless this celebration of Holy Communion that we now want to observe together. May your light shine among us! May your peace be among us. Amen.

28 Dear heavenly Father, we ask you now to give us all your Holy Spirit, and to give it continually, that it may awaken, enlighten, encourage, and enable us to dare to take the small and large steps of moving out of the comfort with which we can comfort each other and into hope in you. Turn us away toward you! Do not allow us to hide from you! Do not let us do anything without you! Show us how glorious you are and how glorious it is to trust and obey you!

We would ask the same for all people, that the nations and governments may bow to your Word, and that they will be willing to work for justice and peace on earth, that your Word may be understood and taken to heart by all those who are poor, sick, imprisoned, troubled, oppressed, and unbelieving; that through word and deed it may be made known to them; and that it may be perceived by them as the answer to their sighs and cries; that all Christian churches and confessions may learn to recognize it anew and serve it with renewed faithfulness; that its truth may be and remain bright here and now in all of humanity's error and confusion, until such a time as it shall ultimately enlighten all people and all things. You are glorified, you who make us free in Jesus Christ, your Son, by confessing and standing on this: that our hope is in you. Amen.

Trinity Sunday: Your People, Your Community

29 Lord, great, holy, and merciful God, you created the whole world. It belongs to you, and it is subject to your will. And so, all people, including ourselves, are yours, chosen by you to give you honor, to use our time and our abilities sensibly, and to be united with one another as your children. In order to remember this, we have come together here on this Sunday morning. We know and are mindful that in all of us, there is much contradiction and resistance, much apathy, stubbornness, and conceit. Forgive us, and do not let us pay the penalty that we would rightly deserve. Break through all the walls that separate us from you and from one another.

Do this now, in this very hour. Grant that nothing false will be said, and that nothing will be misunderstood. Patiently accept our poor praying and singing. We certainly do poorly enough what your angels do rightly. Nevertheless, be present to us and gracious to us. And do this also wherever your people gather on this Sunday. Thus we pray

to you, calling on you in the name of our Lord
Jesus, your beloved Son, using the words that he
taught us:

> Our Father, who art in heaven,
> hallowed be thy name,
> thy kingdom come,
> thy will be done,
> on earth as it is in heaven.
> Give us this day our daily bread;
> and forgive us our debts,
> as we forgive our debtors,
> and lead us not into temptation,
> but deliver us from evil.
> For thine is the kingdom,
> and the power, and the glory,
> forever.
> Amen.

30 Lord, our God, dear Father, we stand in
need, and therefore must be more thankful
in everything, to acknowledge more adequately
and to use more joyfully what you have decided for
us in your great love and done for us in your Son,
Jesus Christ. Help us to surrender all fear that continually results from evil, because your Holy Spirit
says no to it, because through him we are free to
praise you and to love one another without anger.

And now, in your presence, we remember all
those who are not present with us: all the poor, the
sick, the prisoners, and those embattled in any
way; the Christian communities both here and

especially those far away that must suffer and fight for their faith and for ours as well; our entire nation and its government, but also the other nations, and especially the ones that are waging war, and their authorities, with all of the responsibility that they must bear; the heathen, who wait for your Word; and your people Israel, that it too may recognize its King.

Your Holy Spirit is more powerful than all evil spirits. In your Holy Spirit, everything is ordered in consideration and friendliness that today would otherwise weigh heavy on our hearts with unwholesome confusion and brokenness. Amen.

31 God our Father and Lord, here we are, your people, your community, gathered in your presence. We know well that we are a community whom you can rightly reproach for wandering from you, as a whole and as individual members. Yet you have called us in your great mercy, and so we have come to you, to pray to you, to thank you, and to praise you, as well or as poorly as we can. Be among us in this hour! Remove everything false, mistaken, and dangerous, all distraction, misunderstanding, and tedium from our speech and hearing. Open our mouths and ears, and enlighten and quicken us, that we may not just idly speak and listen, but through Jesus Christ, whom you have sent, become doers of your Word and thus people with whom you are well pleased. Amen.

32 Lord our God, we come before you again with the heartfelt prayer that you accept us, that you allow us no rest until we come to rest in you; that you fight both against us and for us until your peace takes its rightful place in our hearts, thoughts, words, essence, and our dealings with one another. Without you we can do nothing, but with you and in your service we can do anything.

Be present and active in all rooms of this house, in this whole city and among all who live in it, and especially among all who are gathered as your community. Be with all the sick and dying, the poor, the oppressed, and those who are lost, as well as those who rule over us and great nations, shape public opinion, and wield the means of power. O that you may bring great love to work against hate, great reason to work against the lack thereof, and not just a few drops but a *stream* of justice to work against injustice! Yet you know better than we do what will be and happen to us and in the world, ultimately ordered to your honor. So we commend all things into your hands. So we, each in our own place and in our own way, desire to put our hope confidently, quietly, and clearly in you. Amen.

33 Lord, our God, you desire that each of us, even today in this house, may hear your comforting and admonishing Word, call on you, and praise you. It is your unmerited kindness that would have it so. For what are we before you and for you? But you have called us, and we have

heard your call. And now we have come together, your creatures, in all the weakness, darkness, and stubbornness that is in us; your children, whom you love, even if we hardly love you or certainly do not love you properly; your community, that both here and everywhere is a great throng, in which you still wish to be present, and with which you still wish to begin something.

And now, we wait, totally directed toward you, for your good Holy Spirit and its gifts. Make this hour bright, pleasing to you, and helpful and fruitful to us! Make it happen from your perspective that what we as people pray, say, and sing has power and truth, comes from our hearts, and returns again to our hearts! Be now our Master and Teacher, a strong, good Lord over all that might happen to each of us in this hour!

In the name of your dear Son, in whom you have shown us your free grace, and will continually reveal it, we pray to you, using the words he has taught us:

> Our Father, who art in heaven,
> hallowed be thy name,
> thy kingdom come,
> thy will be done,
> on earth as it is in heaven.
> Give us this day our daily bread;
> and forgive us our debts,
> as we forgive our debtors,
> and lead us not into temptation,
> but deliver us from evil.
> For thine is the kingdom,

and the power, and the glory,
forever.
Amen.

34 Dear Father in Jesus Christ, your Son, our brother and Lord, you have brought us here together. Stay with us, and go with each of us to our own places when we again leave this place! Do not let go of any of us! Let none of us sink and become completely lost! And above all, let none of us forget you or cease to think of you! And so, enlighten, comfort, and strengthen those dear to us both near and far, our friends and even our enemies!

But we would also like to bring before you all of the known and unknown cares, desires, and needs of all people, those within the Christian community here and in all nations; those who are responsible for consulting, advising, ruling, and deciding in both East and West; those who are downtrodden and oppressed; the poor, the sick, and the old, all those who are troubled, timid, and confused; those all over the world who long for justice, freedom, and peace. Let many, all, and even us learn that we are in the hand of your almighty grace, which will ultimately put an end to all injustice and poverty, in order to make a new heaven and a new earth, in which justice will live!

Glory be to you, Father, Son, and Holy Spirit! As you were in the beginning, are, and shall be, now and forevermore. Amen.

Let the Dawn Come

35 Holy and merciful God, how great is your grace, that you allow us to experience this day and that you bring us together here, in order to call on you and hear your comforting and admonishing Word.

What are we human beings before you? How much vanity, hard-heartedness, and deceit are in our thoughts, words, and deeds! And for that reason, how much error and confusion, how much suffering and need there is, here and in all the earth!

But over all of this, your fatherly heart is open to us, and your hand remains strong, holding us, guiding us, and freeing us. You do not forget or reject any of us. You are near to all of us. You call out to all of us.

Let us take note of this also on this Sunday morning! See to it that what we do here, with our praying, singing, preaching, and hearing, may not be in vain, but would be to your honor, and the awakening, enlightenment, and elevation of us all, for the sake of Jesus Christ. Amen.

36 Lord, our God, this is your inconceivable glory, that we may call on you in this fashion: Lord, *our* God, *our* Creator, *our* Father, *our* Savior; that you know and love all of us, and that you want to be recognized and loved by us; that all of our ways are seen and ruled by you; that we all come from you and may return to you.

And now we spread everything out before *you*: our cares, that *you* may care for us; our fears, that *you* may quiet them; our hopes and desires, that not our will, but *your* good will may be done; our sins, that *you* may forgive them; our thoughts and yearnings, that *you* may cleanse them; our entire life in this time, that *you* may guide it toward the resurrection of all flesh and eternal life. Before you, we remember all who are present in this house, as well as those all over the world who are being held prisoner. Be with our relatives at home, with all of the poor, the sick, the distressed, and the dejected! Enlighten the thoughts and rule the deeds of all those who are responsible for justice, order, and peace, in our own nation and in all nations! Let day break, through Jesus Christ, our Lord. Amen.

Your Good and
Strict Word

37 Father in heaven, you did not leave the world alone, nor did you leave us alone — not as a whole, and not a single one of us. You sought us out and found us, since we had fallen away from you and were lost, by bringing about reconciliation, opening a path to us, and giving us a promise, in your dear Son, Jesus Christ. And now you have given us this Sunday. Now we may come together as his community, in order together to call on you, together to hear your Word, and together to praise you. Look not on our sin, but on your grace. Give us your Spirit, that we may find favor with you. Let us pray to you from the heart, and let your praise come joyfully from our mouths. Especially, let us be upright in what now should be spoken and heard, and take nothing away from what you want to say to us. We pray all of this through Jesus Christ, our Lord. Amen.

38 God, the Father, the Son, and the Holy Spirit, now, let us not depart without your

good and strict Word going with us, each of us to our own place, into our specific experiences, concerns, cares, and expectations, into this whole Sunday and into the coming week! Be and remain present and effective in this house, with all those who live here! Defend against all of the evil spirits that are often too strong for us! Preserve in us the light that so often dies out!

We ask the same for all who gather in your name on this day, whether here or anywhere else, and for the world that so needs a courageous, clear, and joyful Christian witness. We commend to your faithfulness especially our fellow members. We ask you for wisdom for the powerful of the Earth, who by your commission are to care for justice and peace; for sobriety for those who day after day write our newspapers; for love and constancy for all parents and teachers; for a cheerful peaceableness in all families and homes; for open, brotherly hearts and hands for the poor and the forsaken; for relief and patience for the sick; for the hope of eternal life for the dying.

And we thank you that we may spread all of this out before you: before you, who know far better than we what we need and what will best serve your weak church and the poor, confused world; before you, who can and will help us far beyond our asking and understanding.

We are in your hand. We bow to your judgment, and we glorify your grace. Amen.

In Our Work

39 Dear heavenly Father, we thank you that today is Sunday. You now allow us to rest from our work, that you may be able to speak to us and rightly work in us. You have gathered us here through your living Word, our Lord, Jesus Christ. So remain with us and draw us in the Spirit to your Son, that he may draw us in that same Spirit to you. We cannot build ourselves into his community; only you can do that. To that end, hallow, enlighten, and bless our human action, our praying and singing, our speaking and hearing. To that end, reign in our midst. Amen.

40 Lord, our God, you have promised us and instructed us that we may be cheerful in our work, because you have done all things well, because you forgive all our sins, and because you want to crown us on that day of all days with grace and mercy. So let us live from this your Word! We have no other comfort. But your Word is our eternal comfort. Teach us, that we may continually learn to be content with it alone!

We ask that you would remain with your church, both here and everywhere. We pray especially for the church that is tempted, persecuted, and oppressed, and for your embattled people, Israel, all over the world.

We pray for the authorities in our nation, in our city, and all over the world, that you may give them clever, patient, and brave thoughts, that justice, peace, freedom, and faithfulness may return.

We pray for our university, for all of its teachers and students. The fear of you is the beginning of wisdom. Do not take away the light that you once wanted to kindle among us, and that you have preserved for so long, not because we deserve it, but because of your mercy.

We pray for all who have a hard struggle for daily bread. We pray for our youth, for all who are sick and dying, for all who have strayed or are imprisoned, for all who are worried or sad.

Lord, accept your people in grace, help us, and bless your inheritance!

We thank you that we may come before you with all of this and that we may be certain that you have already heard us. Amen.

Instruct Us

41 Lord, our God, in your Son, our Lord, Jesus Christ, you have made us your children. And now we have heard your call and have gathered here together to praise you, to hear your Word, to call on you, and to lay in your hands whatever afflicts us and whatever we need. Be now among us and instruct us, so that all that is fearful and despairing, all that is vain and defiant, even all of our unbelief and superstition, may be made small; so that you can show us how great and good you are; so that our hearts may go out to one another; so that we may understand one another and help each other a little bit; so that this may be an hour of light in which we see heaven open and then a little brightness on this dark earth.

The old has passed, and all has been made new. This is true, and it is true even for us: you are certainly the Savior of us all in Jesus Christ. But only you can rightly say and show this to us. Say and show this to us—to us and to all others who pray with us on this Sunday morning. They pray for us.

And we also do the same for them. Hear them and us! Amen.

42 Lord our God, you see and hear us. You know us, each and every one of us, better than we know ourselves. You love us, even though we truly have not deserved it. You have helped us, are helping us, and will continue to help us when again and again we are about to ruin everything by wanting to be our own help. You are the judge, but also the Savior of all poor, confused humanity. We thank you for that. We praise you for that. And we look forward on that great day to being allowed to see what we are already allowed to believe, if you make us free to do so.

Make us free to do so! Give us an honest, sincere, and active faith in you and in your truth! Give it to many people, to all people! Give it to all nations and all governments, to the rich and the poor, to the healthy and the sick, to the prisoners and all those who think they are free, to the old and the young, to the happy and the sad, to the melancholy and the carefree! There is no one who does not need to believe, and there is no one to whom it has not been promised that "even I might believe." Say it to them and to us, that you are their gracious God and Father, and ours as well!

This we pray to you in the name of our Lord, Jesus Christ. Amen.

Because You Are

43 Lord our God, you find us gathered here to speak and hear your Word, call on you, praise you, and ask you for what alone would make us and the entire world good and wholesome.

But how should this rightly happen? You know just what sort of people we all are, and we know it too. Before you, we cannot deny it anyway: our hard hearts, impure thoughts, disordered desires, and everything that has come of this and still comes of it—our errors and transgressions, and so many words and deeds that do not please you and by which we can only disturb and destroy peace on earth. Who are we, that in this hour we may be able to serve you and really help one another?

Things do not work out without your speaking and working among us. We hold solely to the promise of your grace and mercy, that Jesus Christ, your dear Son, has come to bring good news to us poor, to proclaim release to us captives, and recovery of sight to us blind—to rescue us sinners. But we hold to this promise even in this very hour. You can do what we cannot. You will that it be done. We believe and trust that you will do it—not because we are good and strong, but because you are. Amen.

44 Dear heavenly Father, we thank you. And now, let it happen and be true in our hearts, speech, and actions, that we praise you and agree with you day by day, on this day, tomorrow, and the day after, in the power of your Holy Spirit. Bear with and sustain us henceforth, each one of us. We all need it, each in our own special way. Be and remain the God who is our help, for us, for all who are here in this house, and for all our relatives near and far!

But also be and remain the same above and within the confusing and confused, oppressing and oppressed human actions and events of our days! Say and show to all that they are not lost to you, but that they also cannot run away from you! Show yourself everywhere as the Lord of the pious and the godless, the clever and the foolish, the healthy and the sick; also as the Lord of our poor church, Protestant, Catholic, and all others; as the Lord of good and bad governments, of the well-nourished and the malnourished people; especially as the Lord of those people today who think that they must speak and write either good or not-so-good things; as the Lord of protection for all of us, to whom we are able to commend ourselves, but also as the Lord of judgment for all of us, to whom we are responsible, at the final judgment and already today.

Great, holy, and merciful God, we yearn for your ultimate revelation, in which it will be clear to all that the whole created world and all of history, all people and their life stories were, are, and will be in your gracious and strict hand. We thank you that we may look forward to this revelation. All of this we ask in the name of Jesus Christ, in whom you have loved, chosen, and called us from eternity. Amen.

Evening

45 Dear Father in heaven, we thank you that you have allowed us and commanded us to gather in this hour to pray to you, to proclaim your Word, to hear it, and to take it to heart.

But we are not the people who do this in such a way that it can please you and make us whole. So we offer to you our heartfelt and humble prayer: be among us, and take your cause, even here, into your own hand! Cleanse our speech and hearing! Open and enlighten our hearts and our understanding! Awaken and strengthen our will to rightly recognize you and our readiness to agree with you! Let us inhale the fresh air of your Spirit, that tomorrow we may return to our work with renewed humility, love, and joy!

We here commend to your presence and your guidance not only ourselves, but also all of the other people in our area, in our city, in our nation, everywhere. You have means and ways of speaking to everyone, of comforting them, and of admonishing them. Do not leave them or us alone, that it may be clear, where there is darkness; that there may be peace, where now there is strife; that courage and confidence may grow, where now concern and fear dominate! Hear us, not because we deserve it, but for the sake of Jesus Christ, in whom you, by your inconceivable grace, from eternity, have made us worthy to be your children. Amen.

46 Lord, our Shepherd, we thank you for your eternally new, true, and powerful Word. We are sorry that we so often fail to hear it, or in our dullness or willfulness, that we hear it wrongly. We ask that you preserve it in us, and us in it. We live by your Word. Without its light, we would have no ground under our feet. We depend on your speaking to us again and again. We trust that you wish to do this and will continue to do this, just as you have done it in the past.

In our confidence in you, we may now lay ourselves to rest and take up our daily work anew tomorrow. But in our confidence in you, we also think of all of the other people in this area, in this city, in our nation, and in all nations. You are also their God. Do not tarry and do not stop showing that you are their God—above all, to the poor, the physically and mentally ill, the prisoners, the grieved and the lost, as well as those who bear responsibility in service to the community, whether in the state, the schools, industry, or the courts; and finally, the pastors in this community and elsewhere.

Lord, have mercy on us! You have done it richly. How should we doubt? You will do it richly again. Amen.

At the Grave

47 Lord our God, you give us life, and then you take it away again and hide it for a while in the mystery of death, in order that it may someday be brought into the light, renewed and cleansed, as our eternal life.

Regard and hear us who are gathered here because our brother and friend is now departed from us. Take our dismay and our sadness up in your peace! Take all of our thoughts about the one who has passed on, and about ourselves, into the recognition of your good will for him and for each of us! Teach us to consider that we too must die, and let us be thankful until then for the hope that will not be brought to naught. All this we ask in the name of Jesus Christ, our Lord. Amen.

48 By your judgment, O almighty God, we stand and we fall. Grant that we may rightly recognize our weakness and powerlessness, and let us always consider that you are our strength and power. Help us to let go of all our

reliance on ourselves and the goods of this world. Teach us to seek refuge in you and to put our present life and our eternal salvation confidently in your hands, that we may always be yours and give you honor. Help us learn to rest in you alone and to live from your good pleasure. You are the pioneer and perfecter of our salvation; so grant, O God, that we may subject ourselves to you and follow your call with fear and trembling. Grant that we may constantly call on you and cast all of our cares on you, until finally we have escaped all of the dangers and come to the eternal joy that has been won for us through the suffering, death, and resurrection of your only-begotten Son. Amen.

(After John Calvin)

In You Is Abundance

49 Lord, our God, because we now, at your behest, and in the name of your dear Son, call on you and want to hear your Word, grant that this does not happen without you, but in your holy presence, in the power of your Spirit, and to your glory! We know and confess that there is nothing good in us. But we hold to the fact that in you is abundance. We ask that you awaken within us obedience that makes us useful proclaimers and hearers of your Word; that nothing of its strength, depth, and clarity will get lost because of any fault of ours. We ask the same for all congregations that have gathered at this hour and on this day, both here and elsewhere, for the same purpose. We praise you, that we, as your people, know you and may praise you in humility, until all creation shall be revealed before you and will sing the new song in joy in your presence. Amen.

50 Lord, our God in Jesus Christ, your Son, you humbled yourself, that we might be

inconceivably exalted. You became poor, that we might be rich. You suffered and died, and thereby gave us freedom and life. And this—such eternal mercy and loving kindness—is your power and majesty as our Creator and Lord, is the magnificence in which we praise you, and in whose light we, in the days that you still grant us, may live. For that we thank you.

And in the process of thanking you, we come all the more before you to spread out everything that, according to our understanding, is difficult, unresolved, and in our eyes needs help. We ask you in your grace to consider each of us and have mercy on each of us, who can do nothing without you, now and forevermore.

Have mercy on your church on earth in its confusion and scattering, in its weaknesses and errors!

Have mercy on your people Israel in their blindness to the salvation that indeed came first to them and that indeed first went out from them!

Have mercy on the heathen old and new, near and far, and on the godless and the idolaters, on whom your name has not yet, or not yet properly, shined!

Have mercy on the governments and the nations of the earth, on their perplexed search for peace and justice; on all the confusion in our human efforts in science, training, and education; and on all the difficulties in so many marriages and families!

Have mercy on the innumerable hungry and thirsty, the many persecuted and homeless, the sick, both in body and in spirit, both here and elsewhere, the lonely, the prisoners, and all those who are punished by other people!

Have mercy on all of us in the hour of our struggle and death! Lord, because we believe and know that you have conquered and that, with you, we also have conquered, we call on you to show us but the first steps on the embattled path to freedom. Amen.